Mughlai

MW00744602

Amrita Patel

NEW DAWN PRESS, INC.
USA• UK• INDIA

NEW DAWN PRESS GROUP

Published by New Dawn Press Group
New Dawn Press, Inc., 244 South Randall Rd # 90, Elgin, IL 60123
e-mail: sales@newdawnpress.com

New Dawn Press, 2 Tintern Close, Slough, Berkshire, SL1-2TB, UK
e-mail: ndpuk@newdawnpress.com

New Dawn Press (An Imprint of Sterling Publishers (P) Ltd.)
A-59, Okhla Industrial Area, Phase-II, New Delhi-110020
e-mail: info@sterlingpublishers.com; www.sterlingpublishers.com

Mughlai Magic
© 2005, Amrita Patel
ISBN 1-84557-245-9

Published by Sterling Publishers Pvt. Ltd., New Delhi-110020.
Lasertypeset by Vikas Compographics, New Delhi-110020.
Printed at Sai Early Learners (P) Ltd., New Delhi-110020.

Introduction

Mughlai cooking has occupied a very important place in every Indian household. Though it is a legacy of the Mughals, Mughlai cooking is a part of almost all Indian festivals and celebrations.

Mughlai cuisine stands apart as the empress of the Indian range of cooking. It lays stress on, low flame cooking, rich spice and proper presentation. Another important aspect of this type of cuisine is that the use of spices in the meat dishes brings out the flavour of the meat. Lamb is generally used in most of the meat dishes, though chicken biryani is a delicacy too.

The vegetarian Mughlai dishes do not require heavy flavouring and are cooked in such a way that the vegetables retain their crunchiness. One of the great specialities of Mughlai cooking, and a very popular one too, is kababs. These serve as snacks as well as meal accompaniments.

This book lists out the recipes in different sections for easy reference. The method used in each is easy and simple to follow.

The book will be a handy guide for novices as well as experienced cooks.

Contents

Glossary

Almonds	- badam	Caraway seeds	- ajwain
Aniseed	- saunf	Cardamom	- elaichi
Apple	- seb	Carrot	- gajar
Apricots	- khubani	Cashew nut	- kaju
Asafoetida	- hing	Cauliflower	- phool gobhi
		Chickpeas	- kabuli chana
Bay leaf	- tej patta	Chilli powder	- lal mirch
Baking powder	- meetha soda	Cinnamon	- dalchini
Bengal gram	- chana dal	Clarified butter	- ghee
Bittergourd	- karela	Clove	- laung
Black cardamom	- badi elaichi	Coconut	- narial
Black gram	- urad sabut	Coriander leaves	- dhania
Black pepper	- kali mirch	Cottage cheese	- paneer
		Cucumber	- kheera
Cabbage	- patta gobhi	Cumin seeds	- jeera
Capsicum	- shimla mirch		

Curry leaves	- curry patta	Mace	- javetri
Dates	- khajoor	Mango powder	- amchur
Dried ginger	- sonth	Mango	- aam
Eggplant	- baingan	Minced meat	- keema
Fenugreek	- methi	Mint	- pudina
Flour	- maida	Mustard seeds	- rai or sarson
Garlic	- lahsun	Nutmeg	- jaiphal
Ginger	- adrak	Onion	- piaz
Grapes	- angur	Orange	- santra
Green chilly	- hari mirch	Peas	- matar
Green gram	- mung sabut	Peppercorns	- sabut kali mirch
Groundnut	- moongphali	Pineapple	- ananas
Lady's finger	- bhindi	Pistachio	- pista
Lemon	- nimbu	Pomegranate seeds	- anardana
Lotus stem	- kamal kakri	Poppy seeds	- khus khus
		Potato	- aaloo
		Puffed lotus seeds	- makhana

Raisins	- kishmish	Tomato	- tamatar
Red split lentils	- masoor dal	Turmeric powder	- haldi
Saffron	- kesar	Vinegar	- sirka
Sesame seeds	- til		
Silver foil	- chandi ka vark	Wheat flour	- atta
Solidified milk	- khoya	White cumin seeds	- shahjeera
Spinach	- palak		
		Yam	- zamikand
Tamarind	- imli	Yeast	- khameer

Note: *Garam masala - ground spices, usually a mixture of coriander seeds, cumin seeds, cardamoms, peppercorns, cinnamon, cloves and nutmeg.*

Naan

Ingredients

250 gm flour
½ tsp salt
125 ml milk
1 tsp sugar
30 gm yeast
¼ cup butter
½ tsp baking powder
1 tbsp poppy seeds

Method

1. In a large mixing bowl, sift together the flour, baking powder, salt and sugar.

2. Blend the yeast with 2 tablespoons of milk. Warm the remaining milk and add to the yeast with 1½ tablespoons of butter. Mix well.

3. Make a hollow in the centre of the flour and gradually pour in the yeast mixture. Knead well until the dough is smooth.

4. Cover with a cloth and leave to rise for about 2 hours at room temperature.

5. Divide the dough into 8 portions and form each into a ball with greased hands. Cover the dough balls with a cloth and leave for about 15 minutes.

6. Flatten each ball into a circle of about 5" in diameter. Brush the tops with the melted butter and sprinkle with the poppy seeds.

7. Place the dough circles on a greased baking tray and bake at 230° C for about 10 minutes, or until the naan is puffed up. Serve hot.

Gobhi Paratha

Ingredients

---

500 gm wheat flour
1½" piece of ginger, finely chopped
500 gm cauliflower, grated
1 tbsp coriander leaves, finely chopped
2 onions, finely chopped
1 tsp garam masala
2 green chillies, finely chopped
1 tbsp dried pomegranate seeds, crushed
Clarified butter
Salt to taste

Method

1. Grate the cauliflower coarsely. Sprinkle with salt. Keep aside for 30 minutes.

2. Squeeze out the water and mix the cauliflower with the onions, ginger, coriander leaves, chillies, pomegranate seeds and garam masala.

3. Sieve the flour, add 2 tablespoons of clarified butter, salt and enough water to make a stiff dough.

4. Divide into 6 portions and roll into thick round circles. Place a little of the cauliflower mixture in the centre, seal the edges.

5. Form into a ball and then roll out as thin as possible without letting the stuffing break through.

6. Heat a frying pan and roast these parathas on both sides, adding a little clarified butter, till evenly browned.

Piaz Ki Roti

Ingredients

500 gm wheat flour
A pinch of baking powder
3 onions, finely chopped
A sprig of curry leaves, finely chopped
6 green chillies, finely chopped
1 tbsp coriander leaves, coarsely chopped
Clarified butter
Salt to taste

Method

1. Add the onions, curry leaves, green chillies and coriander leaves to the wheat flour.

2. Add a pinch of baking powder, salt and enough water to make a thick batter of pouring consistency.

3. Heat a frying pan and then lightly grease it. Pour enough batter to cover it thinly.

4. Pour a little clarified butter around the edges. Flip and brown both the sides. Serve hot.

Keema Paratha

Ingredients

---

500 gm wheat flour
225 gm minced meat
1 tsp coriander powder
½ tsp chilli powder
1 onion, finely chopped
1 tsp garam masala
Clarified butter
Salt to taste

Method

1. Parboil the minced meat and keep aside.
2. Heat 2 tablespoons clarified butter and lightly fry the onion.
3. Add the coriander powder, chilli powder, garam masala and salt. Fry till brown.
4. Add 2 tablespoons of water and simmer till the mixture is tender and dry. Mix the meat well with this.
5. Sieve the flour with salt, rub a little clarified butter and add enough water to make a soft dough.
6. Divide into 16 portions and roll out each portion into a thin circle.
7. Spread a little of the meat mixture on one circle and place another rolled out circle on top.
8. Fold the edges of both the circles together.
9. Heat a little clarified butter in a frying pan.
10. Roast the stuffed parathas on both sides till crisp and golden brown.
11. Serve with chutney.

Pulau with Onions and Almonds

Ingredients

---

1 tbsp oil
2 medium onions, thinly sliced
250 gm rice, washed
2 tbsp raisins
2 cups water
1 tbsp almonds, finely, cut
½ cup fresh coriander, chopped
2 tbsp fresh chives or oregano, chopped
Salt and pepper to taste

Method

1. Heat the oil in a heavy-bottomed pan and cook the onion, covered, over low heat, stirring occasionally, for 20 minutes.

2. Add the rice and raisins, then stir for 2-3 minutes. Pour in the water and bring to the boil; cover and cook for 20 minutes (for white rice) or 30-40 minutes (for brown rice).

3. Meanwhile, toast the almonds; spread in a dry frying pan and place over low heat until the nuts turn golden brown. Set aside.

4. When the rice is cooked, add the almonds, coriander, and chives or oregano; toss lightly to combine. Season to serve, garnish with the oregano, if desired.

Chicken Biryani

Ingredients

250 gm basmati rice, soaked in water for 30 min
1½ kg chicken
1 large onion, thinly sliced
2 tomatoes, sliced
2 hard-boiled eggs, sliced (optional)
1 tbsp garam masala
5 tbsp curd
150 ml water
Salt to taste

Method

1. Wash, skin and cut the chicken into medium-size pieces.
2. Sauté the sliced onion in a large pan. Sprinkle the garam masala and salt. Add the chicken pieces and water.
3. Bring to the boil, cover and simmer until the chicken is tender and cooked.
4. Remove the chicken pieces from the stock and mix in the curd. Boil this stock until it is reduced by one-third. Pour this over the chicken pieces.
5. Drain the rice and partially cook in 600 ml of boiling salted water for 4 minutes. Drain the starch water thoroughly.
6. Spread the partially-cooked rice over the chicken mixture. Cook in a moderate oven at 180° C for 30-40 minutes. Serve hot, garnished with the sliced tomatoes and hard-boiled eggs.

Kesari Chawal

Ingredients

500 gm basmati rice
1 medium onion, sliced
1 small pod of garlic, crushed
100 gm clarified butter
1 tsp tumeric powder
1 tsp cumin seeds
½ tsp saffron soaked in 1 tbsp hot water
1 litre water
Salt to taste

Method

1. Wash the rice well.
2. Heat the clarified butter in a heavy saucepan. Fry the onion till it turns soft.
3. Add the garlic, turmeric powder and cumin seeds and mix well.
4. Add the rice and stir well. Add the saffron along with the water.
5. Then add the water and salt, cover and simmer till the rice is done.
6. Serve hot.

Vegetable Biryani

Ingredients

225 gm basmati rice
4 onions, finely sliced
½ kg of mixed vegetables
1 bay leaf, 5 tbsp clarified butter
½ tsp each of white cumin seeds and chilli powder
2 tbsp each of coriander and mint leaves, chopped
50 gm cashew nuts, fried
1" piece of ginger, 30 gm raisins
8 cloves garlic
4 each of green chillies, cloves and cardamoms
2 tsp coriander powder
2" piece of cinnamon
Salt to taste

Method

1. Wash, clean and soak the rice for 15 minutes.
2. Heat the clarified butter, add the white cumin seeds and bay leaf.
3. Add the sliced onion and fry till light brown.
4. Add the spices and fry for 2 minutes.
5. Add the mint and coriander leaves.
6. Drain the rice well and add to the pan. Fry well.
7. Add the mixed vegetables and stir the mixture.
8. Add little more than double the amount of water. Bring to the boil, then lower the flame and simmer till the rice is done.
9. Garnish with the cashew nuts and raisins.

Prawn Pulao

Ingredients

---

225 gm basmati rice
225 gm large prawns
4 tbsp clarified butter
1 cup curd
2 spring onions, finely chopped
3 tomatoes chopped
1½ tsp garlic-ginger paste
2 tbsp red chillies, ground to a paste
1 yellow pepper, seeded and sliced
Salt to taste

Method

1. Heat the oil in a heavy-bottomed saucepan. Add the onion, and garlic-ginger paste and fry for 3 minutes, stirring constantly.

2. Add the tomatoes, red chilli paste, yellow pepper and prawns. Cook till the prawns are done.

3. Add the curd and cook till the smell of curd goes away.

4. In a separate saucepan add water and cook the rice till it is half done. Drain off the water.

5. Add the rice in the prawns and mix. Reduce heat and cook until the rice is tender.

Dilkhush Pulao

Ingredients

250 gm basmati rice
4 onions, sliced
4 cloves
2" piece of cinnamon
4 cardamoms, 4 tbsp ghee
1 tsp red chilli powder
½ apple, diced
2 slices of pineapple
2 tbsp seedless grapes
50 gm almonds, pista and cashew nuts
1 cup fresh orange juice
½ litre water
Salt to taste

Method

1. Clean the rice and soak in water for 15 minutes.
2. Pour the clarified butter in a deep vessel and fry the onions.
3. When the onions are brown, add the chilli powder. Then add the cloves, cinnamon and cardamom.
4. Stir the orange juice in ½ litre water and pour over the rice. Bring it to the boil and then lower the flame. Let it simmer.
5. When the rice is semi-cooked, add the diced apple, pineapple, grapes and nuts. Cook till done. Serve hot.

Fish Pulao

Ingredients

350 gm basmati rice (soaked for 1 hour)
1 large fish (cleaned and cut into pieces)
3 large onions, sliced
Juice of ½ lemon, ½ coconut
5 tbsp of clarified butter
Salt to taste

For the paste

1 tsp coriander seeds, roasted
2 dry red chillies
1 tsp cumin seeds
½ tsp turmeric powder
4 cloves

60 gm desiccated coconut
1" piece of ginger
A bunch of coriander leaves

Method

1. Grate the coconut and boil it in 1 cup water for 15 minutes. Strain this mixture and keep the coconut milk aside.
2. Ground all the ingredients for the paste. Heat 3 tablespoons clarified butter in a pan and fry the ground paste till it becomes slightly red in colour.
3. Add the fish pieces and salt and cook till tender.
4. Heat 2 tablespoons clarified butter in a wok, and fry the onions till brown.
5. Add the drained rice, salt and mix well.
6. Pour in the fish gravy, coconut milk, lemon juice and cook over a medium flame till the rice is almost cooked.
7. Arrange all the fish pieces on top, cover and cook over a low flame for ten more minutes. Serve hot.

Mango Pulao

Ingredients

725 gm basmati rice
3 medium-sized green mangoes
1½ cups coconut, grated
1 tbsp black gram or whole green gram
4 tbsp clarified butter
1 tsp mustard seeds
1 tsp cumin seeds
A little turmeric powder
A few curry leaves
A few green chillies
Salt to taste

Method

1. Boil water in a container. Clean the rice and put it into the boiling water. When it is three-quarters cooked, remove from the fire and drain the excess water.

2. When the rice cools, add the turmeric powder and half the clarified butter. Mix well.

3. Peel, cut and grate the mangoes.

4. Grind the cumin seeds, half the green chillies and coconut.

5. Mix it with the grated mango and then add to the rice.

6. Heat the remaining oil in a pan and add the mustard seeds. When they begin to splutter, add the black gram, curry leaves and the remaining chillies.

7. Add this to the rice and stir well. Serve hot.

Rice with Meatballs

Ingredients

---

250 gm basmati rice
½ kg minced meat
2 large onions
½ tbsp ginger-garlic paste
½ tbsp poppy seeds
½ cup curd
½ cup oil
½ tbsp almonds, blanched
1 tbsp garam masala
Salt to taste

Method

1. Add salt to the minced meat. Wash and squeeze out all the water.
2. Grind the spices and also the almonds.
3. Peel and cut one onion, grind with the minced meat. Keep aside. Slice the other onion.
4. Heat the oil and fry the sliced onion. Add the curd. Cook over a low flame.
5. Form meatballs out of the minced meat mixture and put them in the curd gravy. Keep stirring to avoid scorching. Add the garam masala. Stir.
6. Parboil the rice and drain.
7. In a large pot, spread a layer of rice. Alternate with a layer of meat balls. Keep layering till all is used. Cook over a high flame for 2 minutes, lower the flame and cook for 5 minutes more.

Spiced Rice in Cabbage Leaves

Ingredients

---

225 gm long-grain rice
2 tbsp each of sunflower oil and olive oil
1 onion, finely chopped
2 cloves of garlic, crushed
1 tsp each of cumin seeds and ground coriander
½ tsp fenugreek
125 gm mushrooms, sliced
1 red pepper, diced
300 ml vegetable stock, 5 ml Tabasco sauce
6 Cabbage leaves, blanched in salted water
125 gm cubed mozzarella
Salt and pepper to taste

Method

1. Heat the olive oil and fry the onion and garlic until soft. Add the spices, and stir-fry for 2 minutes. Stir in the mushrooms and red pepper and fry for another 3 minutes.

2. Add the rice and season. Pour in the stock mixed with the Tabasco sauce. Stir, then simmer, covered for 30 minutes.

3. Preheat the oven to mark 190°C. Heat the sunflower oil and fry the bacon until crispy. Stir into the rice with mozarella.

4. Place the mixture on the cabbage leaves, fold the edges with a cocktail stick. Place on a baking sheet and bake for 10-15 minutes. Serve hot.

Malai Masaledaar Ande

Ingredients

6 eggs, hard-boiled
½ tsp garam masala
150 ml cream
2 tbsp clarified butter
2 medium-sized onions
1" piece ginger
A few coriander leaves, coarsely chopped
4 green chillies
Salt to taste

Method

1. Shell the eggs and halve lengthwise.
2. Grind the onions, ginger and green chillies to a paste.
3. Heat the clarified butter in a saucepan and fry the paste for a minute.
4. Put in the eggs and fry till the masala turns pale brown.
5. Add the cream and salt.
6. Add the coriander leaves and simmer till the gravy thickens.
7. Before serving, sprinkle with the garam masala.

Ande Ka Korma

Ingredients

6 eggs, boiled
2 tbsp almonds, coarsely chopped
6 medium onions, finely chopped
3 tbsp clarified butter
1 cup curd
Salt to taste

For the paste

3 green chillies
6 cloves
1" piece of cinnamon
3 tbsp coriander powder
2 cardamoms

½ tsp turmeric powder
1" piece of ginger

Method

1. Cut the eggs in halves, heat the clarified butter and fry them until light brown. Remove.

2. In the same clarified butter fry the onions.

3. Grind the ingredients, for the paste. Add all the ground ingredients to the above and cook over a low flame. Also add the curd and almonds.

5. Add ½ cup water and cook for another 10 minutes.

6. There should be a slightly thin gravy. Put in the eggs and salt. When the oil separates remove and sprinkle with coriander.

Eggs with Tomato and Capsicum

Ingredients

4 eggs, beaten
1 large tomato, blanched and chopped
1 large onion, finely chopped
1 capsicum, finely chopped
4 tbsp oil
A few sprigs of mint and coriander, chopped
2 green chillies, finely chopped
Salt to taste

Method

1. Heat the oil. Fry the chopped onions.
2. While they are browning, add the capsicum and tomato.
3. Add the coriander and mint leaves, green chillies and salt to the eggs.
4. Pour it over the onion-tomato mixture.
5. Quickly stir it and let it cook over a high flame.
6. Remove from the fire and serve hot.

Spinach Omelette

Ingredients

75 gm frozen spinach, chopped
397 gm can plum tomatoes, drained
6 eggs, beaten
2 tbsp single cream of milk
2 tbsp sunflower oil
8 cheese slices

Method

1. Cook the spinach over low heat for 2-3 minutes. Drain off excess water. Quarter the tomatoes, discarding the seeds. Set aside.

2. Beat together the spinach, eggs and cream. Heat ½ tablespoon oil in a frying pan. Add a quarter of the egg mixture. Tilt the pan to coat. Cook for 3-4 minutes.

3. Fill the omelette with a quarter of the tomatoes and two cheese slices. Fold and keep warm. Repeat to make four omelettes. Serve with potatoes and sautéed mushrooms. Garnish with lemon, if desired.

Andon Ka Salan

Ingredients

6 eggs, hard-boiled
250 gm onions, finely chopped
1 large tomato, blanched and chopped
2 tbsp ginger-garlic paste
2 tbsp oil
1 tsp red chilli powder
½ tsp turmeric powder
2 tbsp fresh cream
Salt to taste

Method

1. Shell and halve the hard-boiled eggs.
2. Heat the oil and fry the onions till golden brown.
3. Add the ginger-garlic paste and fry for a couple of minutes.
4. Add the chopped tomato, chilli powder, turmeric and salt. Stir till the oil floats on top.
5. Add the halved eggs to the gravy and let them cook until the gravy has soaked into the eggs.
6. Stir in the cream and serve hot.

Ande Nargisi Kofte

Ingredients

4 eggs, hard-boiled
1 green chilli, finely chopped
1-2 slices of bread
1 small onion, finely chopped
1 tbsp clarified butter
Salt to taste

For the tomato sauce

500 gm tomatoes, peeled
½ tsp garam masala
1 tbsp coriander leaves, chopped
1 tsp chilli powder
Salt and pepper to taste

Method

1. Shell and halve the eggs lengthwise. Carefully remove the yolks and keep aside.
2. Crumble the bread slices and soak in cold water.
3. When soft, squeeze and drain the water. Mash well.
4. Beat the egg yolks and add to the mashed bread.
5. Add the clarified butter, onion, green chilli and salt and mix well.
7. Spoon in this mixture into the egg whites.
8. For the tomato sauce, mix all the ingredients and simmer till tender.
9. Place the stuffed egg whites in a flat ovenproof dish.
10. Pour the tomato sauce over the egg whites.
11. Cover the dish with an aluminium foil and bake in an oven at 180°C, till the sauce simmers.
12. Remove and serve immediately.

Boti Kabab

Ingredients

750 gm lean lamb, cut into 1" cubes
6 small onions
A few lemon wedges

For the marinade

1 tsp black pepper
½ tsp turmeric powder
1 tsp chilli powder
150 ml curd
¼ cup oil
2 tsp coriander powder
Salt to taste

Method

1. For the marinade, beat the curd and mix in the spices and salt.
2. Add the lamb cubes and leave to marinate overnight.
3. Cut the onions into quarters and separate each layer of onion.
4. Thread the onion pieces and meat alternately onto skewers. Brush with the oil. Grill for about 5-10 minutes.
5. Garnish with the lemon wedges.

Shami Kabab

Ingredients

500 gm minced meat
150 gm roasted Bengal gram
Oil for frying
5 each of cardamoms and cloves
3 tsp garlic-ginger paste
Juice of 1 lemon
2-3 green chillies, finely chopped
A few coriander and mint leaves, chopped
¼ tsp each of peppercorns
Cinnamon and cumin powders
Tomato and cucumber slices for garnishing
Chilli powder and salt to taste

Method

1. Add a cup of water in a pressure cooker along with the minced meat, roasted gram, all the spices, salt and a portion of the grated onions. Pressure cook till the mixture is soft and dry.

2. Fry 1 tablespoon of the onions until light brown.

3. Grind the pressure cooked mixture along with the fried onions in a processor until a paste forms.

4. Add the mint leaves, coriander leaves green chillies and the remaining onions in the paste. Also, add the lemon.

5. Make small balls of the paste, flatten each into a patty and fry them until light brown.

6. Garnish with tomato and cucumber slices and serve.

Chicken Kabab

Ingredients

1½ kg chicken
Cucumber slices

For the marinade

150 ml curd
1 clove, garlic crushed
1" piece of ginger, chopped
1 tsp each of coriander powder, garam masala and chilli powder
Juice of 1 lemon
2 tsp black pepper
Lemon wedges for garnishing
Salt to taste

Method

1. Wash and dry the chicken. Remove the meat from the bones and cut it into 2" pieces.

2. Beat the curd and mix it well with the rest of the marinade ingredients to make a smooth paste.

3. Put the chicken pieces in this mixture and leave it to marinate overnight.

4. Thread the chicken pieces onto skewers and grill for 10 minutes, until the chicken is tender.

5. Garnish with the lemon wedges, onion rings and tomato slices.

Seekh Kabab

Ingredients

500 gm minced meat
¼ tsp each of cumin and cardamom powders
2 onions, finely chopped
½" piece of ginger, finely chopped
¼ tsp cloves powder
2 cloves garlic, crushed
1 tsp coriander powder
2 green chillies, chopped
1 egg, beaten
1 tbsp oil
A few coriander leaves, chopped
Lemon slices for garnishing
Salt to taste

Method

1. Mix the meat with the onions, ginger and garlic.
2. Add the spices along with salt to the meat mixture. Mix enough beaten egg to bind.
3. Divide the mixture into 8 balls. Flatten the meat balls and thread these onto the skewers.
4. Brush with the oil and place under a hot grill, turning the kababs occasionally, until the meat is cooked.
5. Garnish with the lemon slices and chopped coriander leaves.

Lamb Kabab

Ingredients

750 gm lamb
2 tsp garam masala
1 lemon
1 large onion, finely chopped
2 cloves garlic, chopped
2 lemon wedges
2" piece of ginger, coarsely chopped
¼ cup oil
450 gm curd
4 tbsp malt vinegar
2 tsp salt
Onion rings for garnishing
1 tsp black pepper

Method

1. Cut the lamb into 1" cubes. Squeeze the juice of the lemon over the meat cubes, making sure that they all are well coated.

2. Add half the chopped onion, ginger and garlic to the curd and vinegar along with the spices. Put this mixture in a food processor and process for about 2 minutes, until it is well blended.

3. Pour this over the lamb pieces, cover and keep in the refrigerator for at least 24 hours.

4. Thread the pieces of lamb onto the skewers. Brush them with the oil.

5. Cook till the pieces are evenly done.

6. Cut the remaining onion into rings and garnish along with the lemon wedges.

Bangri Kabab

Ingredients

400 gm minced meat
1 tbsp each of green chillies and coriander leaves, chopped
4 tbsp Bengal gram
1 tsp each of ginger and garlic paste
1 tsp cumin seeds
4 cloves
1 onion, finely chopped
4 cardamoms
1" stick of cinnamon
¾ tsp salt
8-10 black peppercorns
Oil for frying

Method

1. Boil the minced meat with all the ingredients (except the egg, coriander leaves and green chillies) in ¾ cup water for 10-12 minutes.

2. Cook till the water evaporates.

3. Add the coriander leaves and green chillies.

4. When cool grind the mixture to a fine paste.

5. Beat the egg and add to the above mixture.

6. Make small balls of the paste and flatten each into a patty.

7. Heat the oil in a pan and deep fry the patties till golden brown. Serve hot and garnished with the mint leaves.

Spicy Fish Kababs

Ingredients

350 gm white fish
150-300 ml milk
1 bay leaf
2 tbsp fresh coriander, chopped
1" piece ginger, grated
1 tsp chilli powder
4 spring onions, sliced
4 tbsp each of sunflower oil and mayonnaise
125 gm instant mashed potato granules
75 gm sesame seeds
Salt and pepper to taste

Method

1. Place the fish in a pan with just enough milk to cover. Drop in a bay leaf, bring to the boil and simmer for 4-5 minutes. Drain, remove the skin and roughly flake the fish.

2. In a bowl mix together the coriander, ginger, chilli powder, spring onions and mayonnaise.

3. Make up the potato with 450 ml boiling water. Mix well with the fish and mayonnaise mixture. Season well.

4. Take handfuls of the fish mixture, shape each into cakes and coat each one with the sesame seeds. Heat the sunflower oil in a large frying pan and fry the fish cakes for about 4-5 minutes on each side. Serve with any salad.

Lotus Stem Kabab

Ingredients

750 gm lotus stem
3 tsp cumin powder
1 small onion, finely chopped
2 tsp garam masala
1 tsp ginger, ground
¼ tsp red chilli powder
3 green chillies, chopped
60 gm Bengal gram, roasted and ground
1 tbsp ghee
A few coriander leaves, chopped
Salt to taste

Method

1. Scrape and cut the lotus stem into thin slices and boil in salted water till tender. Remove from the fire, cool and mash.

2. Add salt and the garam masala, ground ginger, cumin powder, coriander leaves, chilli powder and Bengal gram. Mix well.

3. Add the chopped onions and green chillies to the lotus stem mixture.

4. With greased palms make long rolls out of this mixture and pass the skewers through them. Grill till light brown.

5. Heat the clarified butter in a frying pan and fry the kababs till golden brown. Serve hot.

Prawn Kabab

Ingredients

250 gm big prawns, cleaned and deveined
2 tbsp vinegar
½ tsp garam masala
2 tbsp curd
½ tsp ground cumin
4 cloves garlic
½ tsp coriander seeds
½" piece of ginger
2 tbsp clarified butter
2 tsp chilli powder
A few drops of red food colouring
Salt to taste

Method

1. Grind the ginger and garlic to a paste.
2. Add this with the rest of the ingredients, except the clarified butter and prawns, to the curd. Blend well.
3. Marinate the prawns in this mixture and set aside for 2 hours.
4. Thread the prawns onto skewers, smeared with clarified butter and grill till golden brown in colour. Serve hot.

Champ Kabab

Ingredients

1 kg lamb chops
¼ kg curd
¼ kg onions, ground
2 tsp garlic-ginger paste
1 tsp garam masala, freshly ground
½ cup oil

Method

1. Wash the lamb chops. Pat dry with a clean kitchen cloth. Pierce all over with a fork.
2. Mix the onion paste, garlic-ginger paste, garam masala and curd.
3. Marinate the chops in this mixture for three hours. It can also be prepared and kept overnight.
4. You can either fry the chops in oil over a medium flame or barbecue them.
5. While barbecuing, brush oil on the chops. Roast till brown.
6. Serve with mint chutney.

Chilli Kabab

Ingredients

1 kg minced meat
2 tsp black pepper
2 onions, finely sliced
12 cloves, ground
2" piece of ginger
1 tsp turmeric powder
12 green chillies, finely chopped
600 ml curd
1 bunch of coriander leaves, chopped
3 tbsp clarified butter
Onion rings and lemon wedges for garnishing
Salt to taste

Method

1. Put the minced meat into a food processor and process till a fine paste is obtained.
2. Fry the sliced onions in 2 tablespoons of clarified butter till golden brown.
3. Extract the juice from the ginger.
4. Tie the curd in a muslin cloth to drain out the liquid.
5. Pour the ginger juice into the meat paste and mix well.
6. Add the curd, pepper, salt and cloves.
7. Then add the turmeric powder, coriander leaves, chillies and browned onions to the meat.
8. Mix well and keep aside for 2½ hours.
9. Make small balls of the meat mixture. Keep aside for 3-4 minutes.
10. Thread the meat balls onto skewers.
11. Dip in the clarified butter and grill till done on all sides.
12. Serve hot garnished with the onion rings and lemon wedges.

Salmon Kababs

Ingredients

225 gm boneless salmon chunks
1 onion, chopped
2 tsp ginger-garlic paste
1 tsp garam masala
2 tsp each of coriander and cumin powders
4 tsp vinegar or lemon juice
½ cup breadcrumbs
1 egg, beaten
½ cup water
Oil
Salt and pepper to taste

Method

1. Take a shallow saucepan and add the vinegar or lemon juice to the water. Bring to the boil. Add the salmon chunks, lower the heat and let it simmer till the fish is cooked.

2. Drain the water and mash the fish coarsely.

3. Heat the oil and fry the onions till soft. Add the ginger-garlic pastes and fry briefly. Now add the cumin and coriander powders, garam masala, salt and pepper.

4. Add the mashed fish and mix well with the above ingredients, till the mixture is fairly dry. Keep aside to cool.

5. Divide the mixture into balls and flatten them into small cakes. Dip each cake in the beaten egg and roll lightly in the breadcrumbs.

6. Heat oil in a shallow pan and gently fry the cakes till they turn lightly brown.

7. Serve.

Palak Paneer

Ingredients

---

125 gm cottage cheese, diced
625 gm spinach
60 gm clarified butter
½ tsp turmeric powder
1 tsp coriander powder
½ tsp chilli powder
½ tsp garam masala
1 tsp salt
1 tbsp cream

Method

1. Wash and cut the spinach. Cook it in its own moisture till dry.
2. When cool, grind the leaves in a food processor and process for 2 minutes.
3. Heat the clarified butter in a saucepan and add the spices and salt. Cook for 5 minutes.
4. Add the spinach paste, cover and cook over a moderate flame for 10 more minutes.
5. Add the diced cheese to the spinach paste. Cook for 5 minutes.
6. Pour the cream on top just before serving.

Palak Aloo

Ingredients

500 gm spinach
200 gm potatoes
½ tsp coriander powder
2 cardamoms
1 large onion, coarsely chopped
1 tsp black pepper
½ tsp garam masala
1 small pod of garlic, chopped
½" piece of ginger, chopped
50 gm clarified butter
1 tsp salt

Method

1. Wash and cut the spinach. Cook it in its own moisture till dry. When cool, grind the leaves in a food processor for 2 minutes.

2. Peel and dice the potatoes into 1" cubes.

3. Heat the clarified butter in a saucepan and add the chopped onions, garlic and ginger. Then mix all the spices and cook for 2 minutes.

4. Add the potatoes and salt. Simmer for 10 minutes until they are soft.

5. Add the spinach paste and cook over a low flame till the oil separates. Keep stirring to avoid scorching.

6. Serve with roti or naan.

Tarka Dal

Ingredients

225 gm red split lentils
50 gm clarified butter
1 small onion, coarsely sliced
600 ml water
2 cloves garlic, thinly sliced
2 green chillies, chopped
1 tsp cumin seeds
1 tsp turmeric
1 tbsp sesame oil
1 tsp salt

Method

1. Heat the clarified butter in a heavy-bottomed saucepan and fry the onion slices till soft and golden brown. Add half of the sliced garlic and cook for a few minutes.

2. Add the turmeric powder and the lentils. Then add the chillies.

3. Fry the lentils over a low flame for about a minute. Add the water and bring it to the boil.

4. Add the salt and boil the lentils over a moderate flame until it breaks down and the mixture is thick.

5. Heat the sesame oil in a small frying pan. When it starts to smoke, add the cumin seeds and the remaining garlic. The garlic should turn brown.

6. Pour this over the lentils and serve immediately.

Lentil and Vegetable Curry

Ingredients

50 gm clarified butter or white vegetable fat
1 onion, finely chopped
2 cloves garlic, crushed
2 tbsp 30 ml curry powder mix
6 cardamoms
½ tsp ground cinnamon
2 bay leaves
100 gm red lentil, rinsed
1 aubergine, cubed
2 carrots, sliced
1 cauliflower, divided into small florets
1 mango, peeled and cut into small chunks
850 ml water

Method

1. Heat the clarified butter or vegetable fat in a frying pan, fry the onion and garlic until soft. Add the spices and bay leaves, then cook for 1 minute.

2. Add the lentil, vegetables and mango and cook, tossing frequently, for 5 minutes.

3. Pour in the water, bring to the boil and simmer gently for 1 hour. Garnish with the bay leaves and serve.

Kadai Paneer

Ingredients

---

500 gm cottage cheese
2 tsp coriander seeds
100 gm capsicum
5 red chillies
2 green chillies, chopped
½ tsp fenugreek powder
2 tsp ginger, chopped
2 tbsp coriander leaves, chopped
4 tomatoes, finely chopped
3 tbsp ghee
6 flakes of garlic, crushed to a paste
Salt to taste

Method

1. Slice the cottage cheese and capsicum into long, thin strips.
2. Grind the coriander seeds and red chillies together.
3. Heat the clarified butter in a pan, add the garlic paste and ginger. Fry over a low flame for a few seconds.
4. Add the tomatoes and cook till they are tender.
5. Then add the fenugreek powder, green chillies and salt.
6. Finally add the sliced cottage cheese and capsicum, and cook till the gravy is thick.
7. Garnish with the coriander leaves.

Dilkhush Kofta

Ingredients

1 cup split green gram
or black gram with skin
3 tomatoes, puréed
2 tbsp cream
½ cup spinach, boiled and ground
1 tsp ginger, chopped
½ cup cottage cheese, crumbled
2 green chillies, chopped
¼ tsp turmeric powder
1 tsp garam masala
2 tsp coriander powder
1 tsp cumin seeds

Clarified butter for deep frying
Salt to taste

Method

1. Soak the gram for 4 hours. Coarsely grind to a paste.
2. Mix with the spinach, salt and cheese.
3. Form 1" balls and deep fry in the hot clarified butter till golden brown. Keep aside.
4. In 2 tablespoons clarified butter, fry the ginger, green chillies, turmeric and coriander powders, cumin seeds, garam masala and salt.
5. Add the tomato purée and fry till the clarified butter surfaces.
6. Lower the flame, stir in the cream and ½ a cup of water and simmer till the gravy thickens.
7. Arrange the koftas in a dish and pour the hot gravy over it. Serve hot.

Khoya Makhana

Ingredients

15 cashew nuts
¼ tsp turmeric powder
100 gm khoya or solidified milk
2 tsp coriander powder
50 gm puffed lotus seeds
100 gm peas, shelled
1 tsp each of cumin seeds and sugar
3 tomatoes, sliced
½ tsp each of dried mango and
ginger powders
2 green chillies, chopped
Clarified butter for deep frying
Salt and garam masala to taste

Method

1. Roast the khoya on a hot griddle till pink.
2. In a bowl pour one cup of water and add the sugar. Boil the peas in it till soft.
3. Deep fry the cashew nuts and lotus seeds separately, drain and keep aside.
4. Heat 3 tablespoons clarified butter in a pan.
5. Fry the cumin seeds, then add the ginger powder, green chillies, turmeric, coriander and mango powders, garam masala and salt.
6. Add the khoya, sliced tomatoes and boiled peas and cook for 5 minutes, stirring frequently.
7. Lower the flame, add half a cup of water, the fried lotus seeds and cashew nuts. Simmer for 5 minute before removing from the fire.

Khoya-Matar Special

Ingredients

150 gm khoya, crumbled
½ tsp cumin seeds
1½ cups green peas, boiled
¼ tsp chilli powder
2 each of onions and green chillies
¼ tsp garam masala powder
2 tomatoes, puréed
1" piece of ginger
2 tbsp clarified butter
1 cup water
A few cashew nuts
Salt to taste

Method

1. Grind the green chillies, ginger and cumin seeds to a paste. Grind the onions separately.

2. Heat the clarified butter in a pan. Add the onion paste and fry till light brown. Add the khoya (keeping aside a little for garnishing). Cook over a low flame till the khoya turns light brown.

3. Add the ginger-garlic paste and cook for a minute. Add the cashew nuts and sauté for a minute.

4. Add the tomato purée and sauté till the clarified butter floats on top. Add the green peas and cook for 2 to 3 minutes.

5. Add the water, red chilli and garam masala powders and salt. Cook till the gravy is thick.

6. Garnish with the grated khoya, cashew nuts and green peas. Serve hot.

Aloo Gobi

Ingredients

1 small cauliflower
1 tsp chilli powder
½ tsp turmeric powder
900 gm potatoes
½ tsp ground ginger
2 onions, finely sliced
2 tsp coriander powder
100 gm clarified butter
450 ml water
1½ tsp garam masala
Salt to taste

Method

1. Wash the cauliflower and cut into florets, trimming away any leaves. Peel and cut the potatoes into small cubes.

2. Heat the ghee in a large saucepan and fry the sliced onions. Add the chilli powder, ground ginger and coriander powder. Sprinkle with salt.

3. Add the potatoes and cauliflower and gently stir, so that the spices mix well.

4. Lower the flame and cook the vegetables in its own moisture.

5. Cover and cook till the vegetables are tender.

6. Add the garam masala and cook till the mixture is dry. Serve hot with naan.

Dhania Murgh

Ingredients

1 medium chicken, cut into
medium-size pieces
1 tsp turmeric powder
600 ml curd
5 green chillies, slit into 2 each
250 gm khoya or thickened milk
4 tbsp clarified butter
600 ml coconut milk extract
2 large bunches of coriander leaves, chopped
6 cloves garlic
1½" piece of ginger
60 gm each of almonds and raisins
Salt to taste

Method

1. Grind the ginger and garlic to a paste and coat the chicken pieces with it.
2. Heat the clarified butter in a saucepan and fry the chicken pieces till evenly browned. Drain and keep aside.
3. Blend the curd and khoya together to a smooth paste. Mix the turmeric powder and salt. Blanch and slice the almonds.
4. Reheat the clarified butter and fry the almonds and raisins. Add the curd mixture and fried chicken and cook over a low flame till dry.
5. Add the slit green chillies, chopped coriander leaves and coconut milk and bring to the boil.
6. Reduce the flame and simmer without stirring till the chicken is tender and the clarified butter surfaces.
7. Serve hot with plain rice.

Chicken-Do-Piaza

Ingredients

1 medium chicken, cut into pieces
6 cloves garlic
500 gm onions, finely sliced
6 dry red chillies
750 gm tomatoes
1" piece of ginger
1½ tbsp coriander powder
½ tsp each of peppercorns and saffron dissolved in 1 tbsp hot milk
1 tbsp cumin seed powder
600 ml water
4 tbsp clarified butter
Salt to taste

Method

1. Grind the coriander powder, cumin powder, garlic, chillies and ginger in a grinder.
2. Peel and slice the tomatoes and potatoes.
3. Heat the clarified butter in a heavy saucepan and fry the onions till tender.
4. Add the ground spices, peppercorns, tomatoes and mix well. Cook till the gravy becomes thick.
5. Add the chicken and fry for 10 minutes.
6. Add the water and saffron dissolved in milk. Cover and simmer till the chicken is tender and done.
7. Serve hot with naan.

Palak Murgh

Ingredients

1 medium chicken, cut into pieces
2 onions, sliced
500 gm spinach, chopped
4 cloves garlic, crushed
2 tomatoes, finely chopped
2 cloves
2 tbsp clarified butter
1 tsp coriander powder
½ tsp black pepper
4 tbsp whipped cream
Salt to taste

Method

1. Wash and finely cut the spinach.
2. Heat the clarified butter in a pan and lightly fry the sliced onions and crushed garlic.
3. Add the cloves, coriander powder, pepper, tomatoes and spinach and cook for 5 minutes.
4. Add the chicken pieces and salt. Cover and cook over a low flame till the chicken is tender.
5. Pour the whipped cream on top just before serving.

Chicken Korma

Ingredients

1½ kg chicken, cooked till tender and cut into 8 pieces
½ tsp each of turmeric powder
7 green cardamom pods
4 tbsp clarified butter, or sunflower oil
2 onions, peeled and chopped
2" piece root ginger, chopped
5 cloves garlic, peeled and crushed
5 cloves, 1 cinnamon stick
½ tsp nutmeg, freshly grated
¼ gm almonds, ground
600 ml natural yogurt
2 tbsp coriander, freshly chopped
1 tbsp lemon juice
Salt and pepper to taste

Method

1. Reserve the stock of the chicken. Skin the chicken pieces and keep covered.

2. Heat the clarified butter or oil in a frying pan, add the onions and fry for 10-15 minutes until golden. Remove and drain on kitchen paper and reserve.

3. Add the ginger to the frying pan with the garlic, turmeric, cloves, cinnamon stick, cardamom pods and nutmeg. Continue to fry the spices for 5 minutes, then stir in the almonds.

4. Add the yogurt and 150 ml reserved chicken stock and simmer gently. Cook for 15 minutes, or until the mixture has reduced and is of a thick consistency.

5. Return the onions to the pan, together with the chicken pieces and a further 150 ml chicken stock. Add the pepper to taste, then stir in the coriander and lemon juice. Serve hot.

Mirchi Gosht

Ingredients

750 gm mutton
3 tbsp coriander seeds
20 red chillies
6 each of cardamoms and cloves
10 flakes garlic, chopped
4" piece of ginger, chopped
2 sticks of cinnamon (2" each)
4 onions, sliced
300 ml sour curd
1 tsp turmeric powder
Juice of 1 lemon
4 tbsp ghee
A bunch of coriander leaves, finely chopped
Salt to taste

Method

1. Wash and cut the meat into 2" cubes.

2. Heat a teaspoon of clarified butter on a griddle. Roast the red chillies. Keep aside. Fry the coriander seeds, garlic and ginger separately, using 1 teaspoon of clarified butter for each ingredient. Keep aside.

3. Heat the remaining clarified butter in a large saucepan and fry the onions till golden brown. Drain and keep the onions aside.

4. Fry the cloves, cardamoms and cinnamon in the clarified butter. Add the mutton, turmeric powder and salt. Cover and cook over a medium flame till the meat is half cooked.

5. Add the curd, red chillies and fried spices and mix well. Cover and cook till the meat is tender. If necessary, add some warm water.

6. Mix in the lemon juice and fried onions just before serving. Serve hot garnished with the coriander leaves.

Mutton Korma

Ingredients

---

1 kg breast of mutton
4 each of cardamoms and cloves
7 tbsp clarified butter
2 tsp garlic-ginger paste
250 gm onions, coarsely chopped
600 ml curd
2 tsp coriander powder
½ tsp red chilli powder
½ tsp turmeric powder
2 bay leaves
2" piece of cinnamon
Salt to taste

Method

1. Wash and cut the mutton into 1½" pieces. Add garlic-ginger paste, coriander, turmeric and red chilli powders and salt. Mix well and keep aside.

2. Heat the clarified butter, add the onions and fry until brown.

3. Add the meat, along with the cardamoms, cloves, curd, cinnamon and bay leaves. Cook for 5 minutes and add 1 cup of water.

4. Cook till the meat is tender, stirring occasionally.

5. The gravy should not be too thick.

6. Add a little more water if required and cook till the meat is done.

7. Serve hot.

Masaledar Gosht

Ingredients

500 gm mutton
300 ml curd
1 large onion, finely sliced
6 peppercorns
1½" piece of ginger, chopped
3 pieces of cinnamon
10 cloves garlic, chopped
2 cardamoms
3 dry red chillies
4 cloves
1 tsp turmeric powder
2 tbsp clarified butter
Salt to taste

Method

1. Wash the meat and cut into 1½" cubes.
2. Heat the clarified butter in a saucepan and add the onions. Fry them till they turn brown.
3. Add the meat and all the other ingredients.
4. Seal the saucepan with a tight lid and cook over a low flame for about 45 minutes. There is no need to add water.
5. Unseal the saucepan, add more clarified butter and fry uncovered, till the meat is tender and reddish brown in colour.
6. Serve hot.

Mughlai Lamb Chops

Ingredients

---

8 lamb chops
8 cloves garlic
2 medium potatoes
150 ml lemon juice
2" piece of ginger
2 medium onions, sliced
6 red chillies
1 tsp turmeric powder
8 tbsp clarified butter
Salt to taste

Method

1. Grind the ginger, garlic, chillies and turmeric powder to a paste. Mix the lemon juice and salt.

2. Pound the lamb chops gently to shape and soften them. Add the above paste to it and marinate for a few hours.

3. Heat about 8 tablespoons of clarified butter in a deep frying pan and fry the chops until brown. Drain and keep aside.

4. Parboil the potatoes and slice them in rounds. Fry the potato slices in the remaining clarified butter in the frying pan.

5. Fry the sliced onions in the same clarified butter

6. Serve the chops with the potatoes, garnished with the onions.

Rogan Josh

Ingredients

900 gm boned shoulder of lamb, cut into 1" cubes
10 cardamom pods, 2 bay leaves
3 tbsp vegetable oil
6 cloves, 10 black peppercorns
½ tsp ground cinnamon
1 onion, sliced
4 cloves garlic, sliced
1" piece root ginger, peeled and finely grated
4 tbsp water
1 tsp ground coriander, 2 tsp ground cumin
1 tbsp paprika
½ tsp each of garam masala and cayenne pepper

150 ml natural yogurt
Fresh coriander for garnishing
Salt to taste

Method

1. Heat the oil in a pan and cook the lamb until its turn brown. Drain and set aside. Add the cardamom, bay leaves, cloves and peppercorns to the pan and cook for a few minutes. Add the cinnamon and onion and cook until soft.

2. Stir in the garlic, ginger and water and cook until the mixture simmers. Add the coriander, cumin, paprika, cayenne and salt. Return the lamb to the pan and toss to coat the pieces in the spices. Cook for 1 minute.

3. Stir in the yogurt, a little at a time, and the garam masala. Add 300 ml cold water and bring to the boil. Reduce heat, cover and simmer for about 1 hour.

4. Remove the lid and boil rapidly. Spoon off any fat, then transfer to a serving dish. Serve garnished with coriander.